The Giraffe Ma[...] Her Laugh

The cat just sat.

But the giraffe made her laugh.

The sheep went to sleep.

The cat just sat.

But the giraffe made her laugh.

The cow took a bow.

The sheep went to sleep.

The cat just sat.

But the giraffe made her laugh.

The snake baked a cake.

The cow took a bow.

The sheep went to sleep.

The cat just sat.

But the giraffe made her laugh!